Physical Maps

BY SIMON ROSE

The Child's World®
childsworld.com

Published by The Child's World®
1980 Lookout Drive • Mankato, MN 56003-1705
800-599-READ • www.childsworld.com

Photographs ©: Shutterstock Images, cover
(background), 1, 6, 9, 18; Piotr Przyluski/
Shutterstock Images, cover (foreground);
People Images/iStockphoto, 5; Fang
Xia Nuo/iStockphoto, 11; Olesia Bilkei/
Shutterstock Images, 12; iStockphoto, 15;
Africa Studio/Shutterstock Images, 17

ISBN Hardcover: 9781503827707
ISBN Paperback: 9781622434510
LCCN: 2018944819

Printed in the United States of America
PA02397

ABOUT THE AUTHOR

Simon Rose has written 15 novels and more than 80 nonfiction books. He has always been fascinated by maps, especially ones showing the world in different historical periods.

TABLE OF CONTENTS

CHAPTER ONE

What Are Physical Maps?

You and your family are going to the state park.

You look at a map of the park. You see **symbols** for

rivers and mountains. You see a big blue oval for a lake.

You cannot wait to see the real lake!

Physical maps help guide hikers in large areas such as forests.

Physical maps show natural features.

Physical maps show the location of natural features such as rivers, lakes, and mountains. They can show plains, deserts, and forests, too. They also show us how far these features are from each other.

Some physical maps do not show roads or other **manmade structures**. Some do not show **boundaries** of countries or states. They might show major cities.

You can use a physical map to find the natural features on Earth. You can use the map to learn more about a certain part of the world. You can also learn more about the area near your home.

If you live near mountains, a lake, or a river, you can use a physical map to learn their names. If you live near the ocean, you can learn more about the nearby **coastline**.

High
Elevation

Low
Elevation

This is a physical map. It shows information about the landscape of North America.

CHAPTER TWO

Physical Map Features

You can look at physical maps in books, on large posters, or online. You can find them in an **atlas**. An atlas is a book that is all about maps. It can contain many kinds of maps.

Physical maps can show the whole world. They can also show countries or small local areas. They can help us learn about places far away and nearby.

Students who study physical maps in school can learn about other places around the world.

Checking the elevation on a physical map before going on a hike can help show how hard your hike will be.

Physical maps show the **elevation** of different parts of the earth. Elevation is how high an area is above **sea level**. This is shown in different colors on physical maps. The elevation also helps you identify different physical features. You can see **plateaus** or plains on a physical map.

Elevation and features can help you understand places you have never been. You can guess what kind of weather these places might have. Typically areas with lower elevations will be cooler than areas with higher elevations. You can understand what kinds of animals live there. You can imagine what it is like to live there.

Physical maps have a lot to teach us about the world.

CHAPTER THREE

Reading and Using Maps

Physical maps use symbols to help us understand them. They are shown in a **legend**. A legend is a box on a map that explains what the symbols or words mean. It is also sometimes called a key. On a physical map, the legend also explains what certain shapes and colors mean.

Using the legend will help you understand a map.

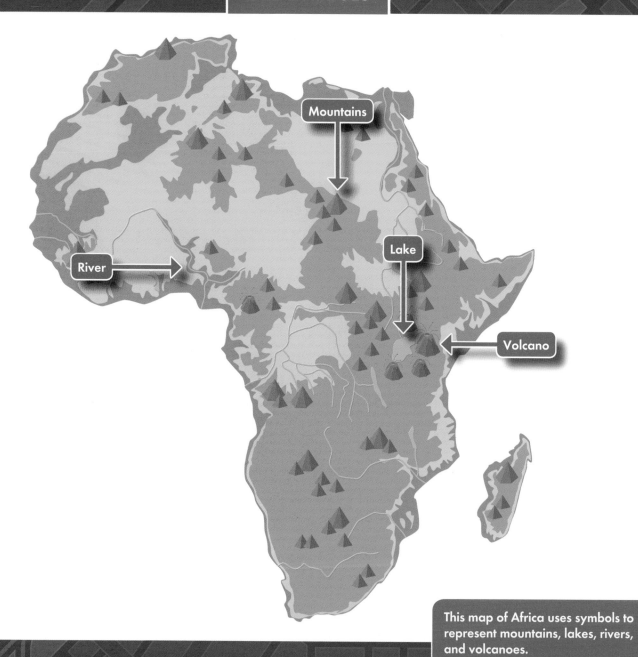

Mountains

River

Lake

Volcano

This map of Africa uses symbols to represent mountains, lakes, rivers, and volcanoes.

On a physical map, colors represent different natural features. Forests are usually colored dark green. Mountains or areas with high elevation are often orange and brown. Low areas might be light green. Plains are usually yellow. Lakes, oceans, and rivers are always shown as blue. On most maps, a city is shown as a black dot. Rivers are shown as lines.

It is important to understand a map's symbols and colors. Then you can understand what the area might look like if you saw it in person.

Do You Know?

Q: What color is used to show water on a physical map?

A: Blue

Q: What color shows forests, and what color shows mountains?

A: Dark green and orange or brown

Q: What are three natural features that might be shown on a physical map?

A: Rivers, lakes, and mountains

Q: When might you use a physical map?

Glossary

atlas (AT-luhss) An atlas is a book of maps. You can find physical maps in an atlas.

boundaries (BOWN-duh-reez) Boundaries are dividing lines that show the end or limit of something. Some maps show the boundaries between states.

coastline (KOHST-line) A coastline is where the land meets the sea or ocean. Many physical maps show where a coastline is.

elevation (el-uh-VAY-shuhn) Elevation is the height above sea level. Areas of higher elevation on a physical map are usually orange or brown.

legend (LEJ-uhnd) A legend is a box on a map that tells what the symbols on the map mean. The legend on a physical map will tell you what the different colors mean.

manmade structures (MAN-mayd STRUHK-churz) Manmade structures are cities, roads, and other things that have been built by people. Physical maps usually do not show many manmade structures.

physical (FIZ-uh-kuhl) Things that are physical have to do with nature or natural objects. Physical maps show the natural features of Earth.

plateaus (pla-TOHZ) Plateaus are areas of high, flat land. Plateaus often shown on a physical map.

sea level (SEE LEV-uhl) Sea level is the average level of the sea's surface against which other heights are measured. Physical maps help us understand how high natural features are from sea level.

symbols (SIM-buhlz) Symbols are designs that represent something else. Maps use symbols to show features on maps.

To Learn More

BOOKS

Bell, Samantha S. *The Purpose of Maps*. Mankato, MN: The Child's World, 2019.

Hirsch, Rebecca E. *Using Physical Maps*. Minneapolis, MN: Lerner, 2017.

National Geographic. *National Geographic Kids World Atlas*. Washington, DC: National Geographic, 2013.

WEB SITES

Visit our Web site for links about physical maps:
childsworld.com/links

Note to Parents, Teachers, and Librarians: We routinely verify our Web links to make sure they are safe and active sites. So encourage your readers to check them out!

Index